The Truth

N. Kerry Mitchell

Illustrated by: Reina Kropf

This book would not be possible without the love and support of my daughter, Kerron Lizzetta Mitchell.

Thank you.

Three things
cannot be long
hidden: the sun,
the moon, and the
truth."

-Buddha

Once upon a
very long time
ago there was a
village called
Verity.

The people of Verity honored truth so
much they decided to build a
monument in the town square.

This would remind everyone how important truth was to them.

After much debate they decided to use gold, because gold was precious and pure. They made a huge block with the word 'TRUTH' carved deeply into it.

The people of Verity were proud of their monument to truth. They taught their children why they had created it and how important it was.

"This is 'TRUTH," they proudly preached. Everyone was pleased.

A few years later, some of the villagers thought that the monument should be updated.

"It's faded and looking worn," they argued. "It needs polished and made brighter. It should stand out more."

Finally, the people decided to wax the monument and add yellow paint in bold stripes.

A few years passed.

After a very bad winter the monument became tattered and dull.

The town once again held a meeting. It was decided to add orange along with the yellow.

So, it was repainted.

Travelers came from many different towns to admire the monument, and so the village grew.

Because the village was growing and so many new people were coming there to live, the town leaders held a meeting. They decided the orange and yellow were outdated and old fashioned. It was time to update the monument!

Most everyone was excited about the new change. There were a few who wanted it returned to gold, but they were voted down. The monument was painted a popular color; a soft shade of blue.

The problem with blue, however, was that it just wasn't as noticeable or as bold as the other colors. Once again, the village Elders called a meeting.

There was much argument over the color this time. After all, there were so many colors to choose from! Again, there were a few who argued that the original gold was best. Once more, they were voted down. This time the town chose a bold red.

This argument occurred every few years.
The monument went from red to purple to
brown to green to. . .

...a rainbow of colors—all at once.

Confused, a little girl asked, "Grandfather? What color is 'TRUTH'?"

It had changed so many times in his life that he had to think—and think—and think.

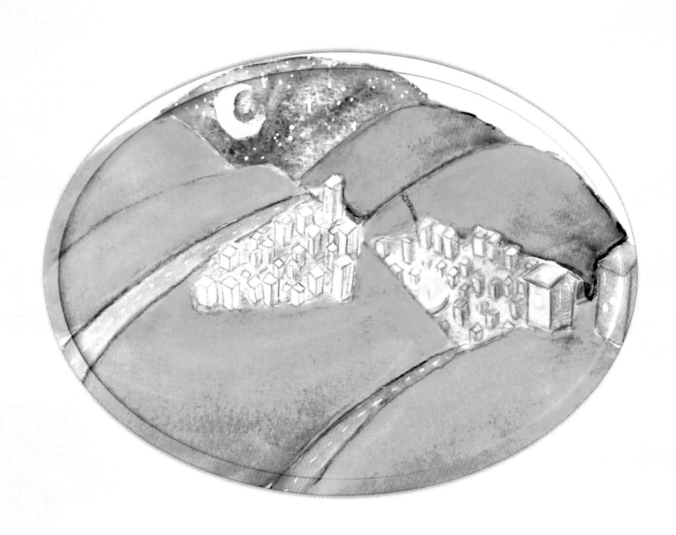

"In a time of
universal deceit –
telling the truth is a
revolutionary act."

- George Orwell

Made in the USA
Lexington, KY
30 April 2019